Something to Think About...

Did you know?

* There are about 2,700 kinds of frogs and toads.

* The largest frog is the Goliath. It is about a foot (30 cm) long.

* Frogs help us by eating harmful insects.

All frogs were once babies called *tadpoles* or *polliwogs*. Tadpoles first look like little fish before they change into frogs. Can you think of any other animals that change completely as they grow from baby to adult?

Frogs

by Robin Dexter
illustrated by Doug Cushman

Troll Associates

Library of Congress Cataloging-in-Publication Data
Dexter, Robin.
    Frogs / by Robin Dexter ; illustrated by Doug Cushman.
        p.   cm. — (Troll first-start science)
    Summary: Simple text and illustrations introduce the habitat,
behavior, and life cycle of frogs.
    ISBN 0-8167-3860-2 (lib. bdg.) — ISBN 0-8167-3861-0 (pbk.)
1. Frogs—Juvenile literature. [1. Frogs.] I. Cushman, Doug, ill.
II. Title.   III. Series.
QL668.E2D52   1996
597.8 ' 9—dc20   95-22524

Hop, hop! *Splash!*

A frog can jump.
Jump, frog, jump!

A frog can swim.
Swim, frog, swim!

A frog is an animal called an
amphibian *(am-FIB-ee-un)*.

Amphibians can live on land *and* in water.

A mother frog lays eggs in the water.
The eggs look like this.

What's inside the egg?

Inside the egg, a baby frog grows.

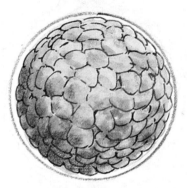

1 day

3 days

A baby frog is called a *tadpole*.

10 days

6 days

Soon, the tadpole leaves its egg.

Tadpoles live only in water.

The tadpole grows bigger. It looks like a little fish!

2 weeks

6 weeks

Then the tadpole grows legs.

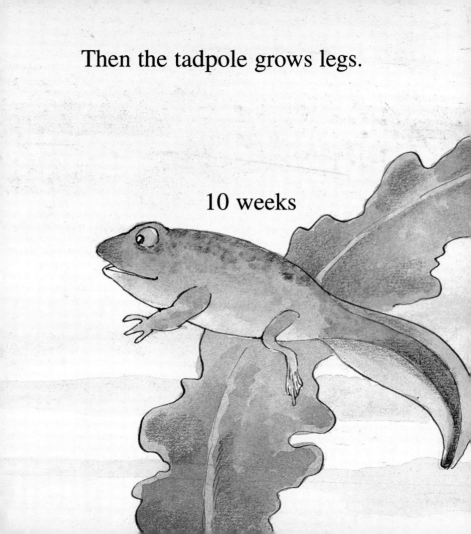

10 weeks

Soon the tadpole grows lungs.
Now it can breathe air.

Then the tadpole loses its tail.

12 weeks

The tadpole is now a little frog!

The little frog can live in water
and on land.

The little frog eats insects,
worms, and snails.

Some animals eat frogs.
Jump, little frog!

Frogs like warm weather.

When the weather is cold,
a frog cannot stay warm.

So during the cold weather,
frogs sleep.

They sleep in the ground
all winter long.

When spring comes, the frogs
wake up.

Frogs like to jump and leap.
That looks like fun!

Can you jump and leap like a frog?